Re-Origin
of
Species

Re-Origin
of
Species

Poems

Alessandra Naccarato

Book*hug Press
Toronto 2019

Library and Archives Canada Cataloguing in Publication

Title: Re-origin of species / Alessandra Naccarato.
Names: Naccarato, Alessandra, author.
Description: Poems.
Identifiers: Canadiana (print) 20190160187 |
    Canadiana (ebook) 20190160209
    ISBN 9781771665421 (softcover) | ISBN 9781771665438 (HTML)
    ISBN 9781771665445 (PDF) | ISBN 9781771665452 (Kindle)
Classification: LCC PS8627.A27 R46 2019 | DDC C811/.6—dc23

PRINTED IN CANADA

The production of this book was made possible through the generous assistance of the
Canada Council for the Arts and the Ontario Arts Council. Book*hug Press also acknowledges
the support of the Government of Canada through the Canada Book Fund and the
Government of Ontario through the Ontario Book Publishing Tax Credit and the Ontario
Book Fund.

Book*hug Press acknowledges the land on which it operates. For thousands of years it
has been the traditional land of the Huron-Wendat, the Seneca, and most recently, the
Mississaugas of the Credit River. Today, this meeting place is still the home to many
Indigenous people from across Turtle Island, and we are grateful to have the opportunity to
work on this land.

Book*hug Press

For survival

Contents

Postcards for My Sister

Per Nozze E Lutto—Si Lascia Tutto
To marry and mourn, you leave everything
(Calabrese Proverb)

Above the green village, a hill where no one lives.
Our great-grandmother is buried there.

Before the town fell, they spread
their cards and drank. Big-mouthed women, fat
as trees, their ceilings hung with meat.

A whistle of us in their hands as they made plans
for weddings and daughters.

Our grandmother spoke to a man on the phone,
and this was how she was married.
Her long blue skirt, two gold front teeth.

On that green hill, I lay down with a man and read.
The floors have turned to moss.

There are no gravestones there.

On Shell Beach, a fawn with broken neck, weeping.
Sophie's hand on split bone, a crown of rocks and seaweed.

I was certain I would mother alone, then calves were born
all spring and our sister arrived to the coast. Nine months

in a busted sedan, crying. Welfare kitchens, our shared father;
we are richer on the road, her mother says, and how

can I argue? We can't expect joy, I tell our sister like you told me.
But that night: algae on the shore, phosphorescence,

we walked into the cold, bright glitter. No one mothers alone
in the end. The fawn on Shell Beach weeps until it is still.

Sophie places a shell on its eye. The water will guide it away
by morning. The tide has its own kind of care.

The small house crowded with women.
The small body you were not ready to leave.

There were no legal midwives, but the women knew
how to turn a child.

Three days, the small house, our mother screaming.
She would not go to the hospital.

We come from this woman,
from women like this.

The plum tree where my friend parked
to sleep with feet in starlight, the night before

the public clinic, where a nurse would count
backwards in time. On the dance floor,

my friend whispered   *it's okay to play gatekeeper*

to past self, to me as I whirled silk into flowers,
small rain of blood at thigh: immaculate re-conception.

Four weeks along, though I'd known
the alcoholic for three. Unreliability of time,

of fathers. The word inside mother: *tergiversari*.
To turn away is to turn to, straddle, go on.

We have always taught each other
how to give birth, and not.   *My same child came,*

she told me under the plum tree. Once her sadness
had spun out and dried: *Rowan was always his name.*

Above the green village, a hill where no one lives.
Our grandmother is buried there.

After the earthquake, they spread
their cards and drank. Big-mouthed women, stern
as orchards, sending their daughters away.

The girls were told to not turn back. Our grandmother
waited sixty years, then packed her suitcase again.

Her second marriage ended with a Greyhound ticket.
In a long blue skirt, two gold front teeth, she left
to pick wild mushrooms.

Before the flight, joked with our mother
about the life of single women.

On that green hill, I lay down in her old scarf.
The grass is bright with flowers.

There are no gravestones there.

Imminent Domains

The breaking up of the terrestrial globe, this it is we witness.
(Eduard Suess)

MOUNTAIN THAT EATS MEN

Cerro Rico, Potosí

When I meet the devil, his name is Uncle. Inside
a silver mountain, the *mountain that eats*

men, eight million tibias rest. The old mine shifts
toward an unknown tectonic, nearly bankrupt.

In the underground den, I chew coca leaves
and leave a fifth of vodka at Uncle's feet. It is hard

not to stare at the figure's erection, white flowers,
his small and mighty horns. Dead of black lung

at twenty, these kind men and our great uncles,
the Calabrese poor. Beneath the Canadian Shield,

they prayed to *Playboy*s and handkerchiefs,
mostly came home. Here, too many widows,

the tourists gawk. I want to slide inside the shaft
of earth as if greeting an old friend.

What do I know about sacrifice? Outside, they
grace the refinery with blood. Two hundred llamas

split belly to sternum. It has been a good year,
they say. It has been a good year in the mountain.

THIS IS HOW YOU MAKE A HAUNTING

It takes three days to panhandle
enough for the bus, and then
your father is already on the shelf
our people use for the dead.

The cat's tail curled around
zucchini stalks, garden purring.
All earthworm and yellow flower,
wet as the day you left home.

Here is the bed. Here is your tag
on the milk-store wall: *Mano Negro*.
Here is your long-haired brother
lifting the cat from the earth.

Hot oil in the pan. Fat mother
at the stove, battering flowers.
Seven years of black cloth, says
she'll learn the language now.

Gives you his coat, the wool
inheritance. Here you are:
thin and shot full of poppies,
black-eyed eldest.

The rock wall leans onto the
highway, you can hear dead river
under your house. Two years
doesn't change the land,

just the body. Where a thorn
pierced your forearm, button
your father's sleeve. Visit his
mausoleum, its sweet quiet.

Your name on the door, blood
inheritance. Put your hand
to the language: here is your body,
here is your way to carry on.

Someday, I'll be that same body,
heaving at the flower's bright stem.
Will need to know how cold
the stone was when you touched it.

How you vomited beside the plot,
shook for days in your old room.
Mother skinning rabbits for soup,
brother holding a spoon of broth
to your small blue mouth.

THE FISH

The story is he gives me a fish.
The problem is my hands only hold so much water.
The problem is my hands leak water.
The problem is I want it to keep living.

The setting is a municipal campground.
The setting is not far from the creek.
The setting is Thursday. Muggy, wet evening.
The smell of burning pine.

We turn away from the fire together.
We walk to his tent where the light is slanted.
This is where he gives me the fish.
This is where I can't unhold it.

The story is he's drunk.
The story is his father.
The story is my body should be able to shelter it.
The body rarely does what it's told.

The problem is I want to keep living.
The problem is my hands are not ponds.
The problem is he wants me to keep it.
The story is I give it back to the land.

LAND THAT ERASES

When I met her, her skin was clear as obsidian glass.
The cabin rocked like a boat as the wind blew through it.
Her body had been an archipelago, kissed white by rash.
Incurable, they said as she prayed the marks from her.
Needles in the meridians, creams of sheep's gut and steroids.
She lived on a cruise ship then. A co-worker leapt from
the ledge as tourists ate dinner. They could not turn back.
Her job was to sell watches and vitamins, so she wore
long sleeves. Then she heard of an island that devoured
parts of itself. Once there was a town and now there wasn't.
Land sold for the price of a watch, that close to the crater.
It lit her kitchen with a soft red glow.

IMMINENT DOMAIN

Fissure 18, Leilani Estates

I have been there in a blue dress, in a blue tent
at daybreak. The boar outside my window
had tusks thick as my wrists,

and lying there pregnant
I held a salamander in my hand. A village,
then another village. And another
village soon, when the lava

is done. A friend named Peter
moved rocks to decorate,
and deep in the night was shaken
by the old wives who guard

that place. We want to be forgiven,
by our mothers and the land: re-colonizer kids,
in our deep kisses and rum. I have danced

with swan feathers in my hair, drunk on the new
self I found, warm and taken. The gash
in the earth laughs, the way planets laugh

at girls like me, at Peter. Pregnant, I scaled
chicken wire at the dump,
touched fresh obsidian. It broke in my hand
like black salt;

I took nothing with me. At the estuary,
my aunt wore a gas mask
and washed her feet. Imminent, eminent domain.

The road remembered itself fire,

the lizard dropped its tail. The tail burned
and the road broke free.

ONE HUNDRED WAYS TO DIE IN YELLOWSTONE

Alcohol poisoning
Approaching wildlife
Arrowhead
Aspen (fall of)
Aspen (fall from)
Aspen (collision with)
Avalanche

Bighorn sheep (horn of)
Bison (charge of)
Bear
Boulder (dislodged)
Brucellosis (bison served in main dining room)

Caldera, supervolcano (accidental entry)
Caldera, supervolcano (entry, push by new husband)
Caldera, supervolcano (eruption)
Caldera, supervolcano (steam)
Choking
Climate change
Concussion (from kick to the head, see: Bighorn sheep)
Coyote attack

Daffodils (consumption of)
Dehydration
Dismemberment (by wildlife)
Dismemberment (by snowplow)
Drowning
Drunk driving

Earthquake

Echinococcus granulosus eggs (through handling of wolf scat)

Elk (stampede of)

Endangered species (attack by)

Endangered species (sale of, resulting in GSW, see: Firearms)

Erosion

Exposure (extreme cold)

Exposure (extreme heat)

Exposure (bad psilocybin in the head cook's cabin)

Falling

Firearms (premeditation)

Firearms (mistaken for deer by wildlife control)

Firearms (see: Suicide)

Forest fire

Forgetfulness

Gangrene

Geyser (bathing in, mistaken for hot spring)

Geyser (falling)

Geyser (diving after family pet)

Grizzly bear (claw of)

Grizzly bear (consumption by)

Hallucinations (sudden onset)

Hallucinations (see: Exposure)

Hemlock

Hitting gas instead of brake

Hurricane

Hypothermia

Hydrothermal pool (see: Geyser)

Icicle (fall of)

Improper storage of food

Infidelity (see: Firearms)

Jumping into thermal pools (see: Geyser)

Kayaking

Landslide
Lightning
Loneliness
Lynx
Lyme disease (see: Climate change)
Listeria

Mountain lion
Moose (kick by)
Monkshood

Narcolepsy

Obsidian rock (fall from)
Obsidian rock (fall of)
Off-road travel by ATV
Oleander

Picnicking in proximity of wildlife
Poisonous mushroom mistaken for chanterelle

Quail (distraction by, while hiking)
Quarter-life crisis

Rattlesnake

Speeding
Snowmobile
STI/STD (contracted in the ranger lodge, left untreated)
Suicide (see: Loneliness)
Sudden collapse of road

Tree branch (fall from)
Tree branch (fall of)
Tree pose (Vrksasana) at the edge of a thermal pool (see: Geyser, Falling)

Unanimous group decision to swim at night, drunk
Unreported injury

Venom (see: Rattlesnake)

Water hemlock (mistaken for parsnip)
Wolf
Wolf scat (see: Echinococcus)
Wolverine pack
Whirling disease (consumption of trout with)
Winter
Wildlife viewing

Xenophobia
Xanax (use of, in presence of wildlife)

Youthful sense of entitlement

Zip lines

IT COULD BE A VIRUS

It could be your mother. Could be the toilet seat
in fifth grade, or wearing your swimsuit all that
sunny day. It could be the fish you ate that swallowed
the worm, or microplastics. It could be that bad pair
of shoes. Herpes zoster, or Herpes simplex, or
cytomegalovirus. Inherited DDT, Fukushima radiation,
copper poisoning, dental amalgams, or chemical injury.
It could be your personality. Your father's silence,
the year your sister would not eat. It could be that time
you were rejected from art school and lost your virginity
after eating bad shrimp. Could be disappointment,
multiple sclerosis, or rheumatoid arthritis. Your malaria
treatment in a clinic with no running water, parasites,
or your tendency to complain. It could be PTSD, or
blood cancer. The tests came back fine. Celiac disease,
arrhythmia, or your refusal to think positively.
It could be the tick that bit your areola, like you
were at a party in Montreal. It could be the wolves
they shot, the deer that overbred, until Lyme disease
went viral. It could be pollution, or loneliness.
Or maybe bacteria. It could all be your fault.

DEFORESTATION

Gulf Islands, BC

It's winter when we decide
to live in a red house by a small lake.

Every time we go to the emergency room
doctors suggest the mountain,

where men have built a monastery.

Blood is fine, blood is thin.
I have a prodigious imagination, endless.

In the red house, you cook fish.

A woman strips by the road and breaks
the ice on the lake to swim.

Lyme, Connecticut

Summer, a red barn where children
rest, their knees

the size of moons. Everything is circular: tick-rash,
their small pink mouths, temporary paralysis.

Doctors say their blood is fine,
as the children remain in bed. They cannot say

acorn, kettle. Can't name their town, soon to be famous
for the disease's vector. Mothers pray

over red cough syrup and the children swell,
pink and dumb, they sleep.

Illinois Mountain Park

Postwar housing, cheap and red. Martha's backyard
built into the national park, just like

her two hundred neighbours'. *Destroy the forest,*

> *and the apex predators vanish*
> *leaving the disease producers and spreaders free rein.*

Contractors ignore ecologists,
ecologists go bankrupt, ad infinitum. Martha's backyard

at the feet of one hundred maples, a dead fox den,
white-tailed deer and deer ticks.

> *We may not have created it,*
> *but we sure as hell facilitated the spread.*
> *30,000 new cases a year,*

if the disease exists. If it's not just in her head,
like the CDC suggests.

> *Aseptic meningitis:* the swelling in Martha's brain
> *of unknown origin,* uninsurable.

Long Point, Lake Erie

It crosses the border. Begins on a sandbank,

in the red morning, a girl laughing
from her tent to swim with her mother.

In this heat, what insect can sleep?
Vector carried north on a warm winter breeze.

Doctors say her blood is fine, just thin,
as she grows into an undiagnosed woman.

The re-abled know climate change is within us:
the zoonotic future, bacterial now.

All glaciers melt with mysteries inside.

Gulf Islands, BC

It is winter when I watch my blood pearl
into test tubes in a complex-disease office.

My blood will fly to Germany on packs of ice.
This is the last time I will ask a doctor to believe me.

I have driven past blue-cut fields in this province,
watched deer nudge split ravens, ravenous.

What happened to my body is a quiet acre of sod.
Deforestation. At dawn,

a woman strips by the road to swim.
I watch the ice on the lake give way to her hand.

Creationisms

From so simple a beginning, endless forms.
(Darwin)

DROUGHTLAND

Under the maple, a blind black cat chews on a chicken bone.
There's a well under us, heaving itself dry. A death over us,
set in white sky. No witch begs for water. The witches piss
on ground so hot it hisses. Carry five-gallon jugs to the root,
bathe cold in the maple's shadow. Point to the vulture,
circling the mountain. To the rattler who no longer rattles.
Curled in the centre of the path, if you're looking for an omen.
A white fox stands ankle-deep in the creek. The bank cracks
loud, dry as stone. I have never been so alone, so thrashed
by a land. Hope is white bone in the beak of a buzzard,
his feast and shit, the fecund turn of nature. First you need
to admit you are dying. Then you can see how the blind cat
gnaws, unafraid of the bone breaking in his throat.

MISCARRIAGE

Hexagons. Forty thousand wings,
weeping against the comb. Dark as inside
the body, dark as unbroken wood.
Working light from their bodies,
sweet geometry dripping like a gland,
a small world's thymus.

> Reaching for an old fling,
> in a damp café; trying to hug
> in the sopping crowd,
> the bee flies between us, barbs
> into bone between my breasts.

Algorithmic, autocatalytic; a scout
dancing his harvest on the floor.
Colony torn open at the sound,
moving to obliterating light, pregnant
crop, crop-dusted and grafted,
that universe of canola.

> Hot cloth, tweezers; the stinger
> just buries deeper. Sometimes nature
> wants you closer, to kiss the blood
> right out of you. I watched a girl slip
> off a mountain; red against the pine bed
> where she split her femur, lucky.

The world is math disguised
as colour. 1 : 1.618 : seed head :
cauliflower : nautilus shell : hurricane :
the reproductive pattern of honeybees :
the ratio of a healthy uterus.

My body weeps at the sting, blue and
swelling, elbow sweat and knee back
sweet. That old fling puts a hand to me
8 weeks later. Pauses as the café
grows louder; worried it was him.

Monochromatic, pulped with dust
the hive can't harvest, colony
still thrusting into seed head,
into smell of light, purpose. Infertility
a compass, white need turning
the queen from her land.

They're on a neighbour's milkweed,
at 13 weeks. 2 land on my wrist, 3,
then 5. They circle the skin, dizzy as suns,
place filigree legs on my saccharine skin.
Eating what nectar they can, until
I shudder; suddenly cramp.

0 yield, 1 scouts toward water, 1 knows
they haven't crossed it before, but 2 follow,
3 crane to the reflection of a flower, 5 land
to drink, 8 flock beneath, plus the 5 is 13,
nature repeats itself, 8 flock under, which is
21 beneath, and then 34 suicides and nature
repeats itself, which is 0 bodies in the hive,
1 gloved hand reaching, 1 keeper vomiting
by the hive, 2 miles from the water.

I wake in a puddle of honey, glistening
at the crotch. The stinger beside me
like a lost earring and everything so quiet
I can hear that girl as she fell, wind
cutting her voice as gravity took
from her what it wanted and there
wasn't anything I could do.

IT'S ABOUT SURVIVAL

Interview with beekeeper Ian Smyth
Downtown Eastside, Vancouver

Humans are the most resilient of all creatures. We adapt
to the shelter, the street. Dive hotels, bedbugs as pets,
random acts of violence. Condos going up; condos going up,
condos complaining about Hastings—or a rooftop garden,
wildflower, hive. Having them crawl all over, wings vibrating
through gloves. You know? There's going to be famine.
Supposed to be, in end times—Mass decline, pesticides,
destructor mites. We're gone within five years of the bees.
Insects aren't just creatures of instinct. They dance
in the dark, collect followers. Tell the hive their source
in relation to the sun. Take off the cover, all of a sudden
it gets louder. You hear them hum, moving slow, deliberate.
They expect us to be gone soon, this neighbourhood
in end times. It depends how you look at it. Which guy
knows how to protect himself best? It's about survival.
In the downtown honey, something you can't name.

COYOTE MEDIA

Walking across the tarmac in Toronto,
twelve of them panting. Small wild dogs
facing big silver birds, as pilots explain
and passengers crane to watch the pack
stalk through the memory of a forest.

My aunt faces her garden, tea steaming
like breath over the Rideau Canal.
Watches a coyote walk through her
yard, deep in drifts, snow to its belly.

My grandfather fed compost to coyotes.
Bones of deer he hunted each fall, scraps
from his garden. Left piles by the stream
once first frost fell, worried the pack
couldn't catch enough in those trees.

By the Sauder School of Business,
I see my first coyote. Yellow-eyed, thin,
so close I can hear him breathing.
Nearby, a dozen students take his
picture—bread in maw—and overnight,
the coyote's Twitter trends.

My grandfather walked through drifts
of winter, even as cancer spread in his
bones. Determined to feed them scraps
and marrow, return what he had to land.

Midway through the yard, the coyote
pauses. Turns to my aunt, dips its snout
slightly. She places her palm to the glass.

It takes nearly three hours for Pearson
to recover. After the coyotes are shot with
sedatives, rounded up by wildlife control,
the pilots try to forget the ferns they saw
rising under the feet of the dogs.

MEDIA COYOTE

as in: to trick, to hoodwink. And it's hoods we're talking about, Dani.
You first made those coats for arctic explorers, whose eyelashes froze
from the wet of their eyes, who needed goose down and coyote fur
on their hoods to survive where their ancestors hadn't, to eradicate
climate change or drill for more oil, whatever the contracts were for.

How many coats can you trim with the fur of one coyote? I'll ask
if I see CEO Reiss. After all, we went to the same high school.
Just wondering, what percentage of the jacket do you pay your
trappers per pelt? When you say you share the values of the North,
do you mean *staying warm*? Or something more applaudable.

Let's be honest, Dani. In Forest Hill, there aren't many trees. Just big
lawns and credit cards, kids with keen fashion. No one cares what
PETA says, so why try to justify the fur? It's a slow, certain death
on those hoods, however you claim it. In our old class, tenth graders
pray for your jackets, but who explains the *total cost*? I bet they mislearn
the Fur Trade like we did. Thanks to your coyote ads, think themselves
invisible within the trim.

SUICIDE SEEDS

We have made a commitment not to commercialize sterile seed.
We stand firmly by this commitment —Monsanto

Inside each seed there is another seed,
this is our closest infinity. Except some seeds

in corporate testing, marked *research*
and *development*. My friend's uncle followed

his fields, to market, to coroner's office.
Body already in repayment: skin blue

with crop dust, life remortgaged twice.
Genetic Use Restriction Technology prevents

seed duplication, not subtraction. More farmers
take their lives than veterans;

suicide rates are the highest of any occupation.
Inheritance carries on until it doesn't,

genetically. Inside each seed there is
often a patented genome. *To even the playing field.*

To protect innovation. If they divided the earth's seed,
four hands would hold it now.

The farmer's hands are one hand.
Our hands are in the farmer's hands.

There are no suicide seeds—sold commercially.
There is only an active patent.

GENERATION EXODUS

I will perform these signs among you
(Exodus 10)

*

I'm working the bankrupt field
when I see them coming:

a thousand thousand mouths
in yellow heat, descending.

"the verdict was wrong   *"the lord said—*
on glyphosate
glyphosate
does not cause cancer

Modification,   Does the grasshopper know
metamorphosis.   what he is becoming?

We sold ourselves to the bank
for a handful of seed, bad acreage.

What did we know about yields?
In cut-offs, gay as a sunrise.

our hearts go out   *I have hardened his heart*
we understand their desire   *and the heart of his officials*

Re-genomed,   Solitude worshipped
desexed and flowering.   into swarm, into reckoning.

We're returning to the land,
we told the agent as we signed
the loan, sub-prime.

Our field sexless, unflowered.
Beige as the home we left,
sallow as our bed.

for answers   *I may perform these signs*
                                 of mine among them

It only takes three   Grasshopper, grasshopper—
for a swarm to begin.   now locust.

My wife by the shallow creek
each morning. She's there

when the sky blackens. Runs
toward me, the field—under the swarm

so quickly, she cannot hear
me shout.

We will appeal   *swarm over the land*
vigorously defend   *devour everything growing*
                                 in the fields

Bang-winged,   Trillions rising
gregarious.   from drought.

The dark metal of the locusts
finds me, as I find her

many hands   lift us
as if we are   *returning.*

science will prevail."   *everything left by the hail."*

Their hunger becomes   How quickly a famine
our hunger.   is reborn.

There is nothing left
for the creditors to claim.

MIMICRY

Earth Coincidence Control Office (ECCO)
St. Thomas, 1964

They built an apartment of glass, filled it with seawater,
and hired a young woman from the beach. She lived there
in shorts, slept on a shelf above the dolphin she was training
to speak English. The dolphin liked to hold her fingers
in his mouth, and she liked to stand in the sun on the flooded
balcony, as if still part of the world. Downstairs, men in
lab coats took LSD. Watched as the dolphin went into heat,
refused to open the apartment door, in the name of science.
There was only one way to calm the dolphin down.
NASA paid for the hand job. NASA paid for the word
they thought was coming. Margaret's name, so close
in the dolphin's mouth. From his blowhole, simulacrum:
nature's code nearly broken into vowels.

RE-ORIGIN OF SPECIES

On our island, nothing
eats us but the rifle.

> A headache like plates
> shifting inside my skull.
> That's how it starts.

> > *"species*
> > *are not immutable*

We own the high wood, breed
the forest crowded.

> IV, three days high. My hard
> body spun cotton. The CT
> shows *unorthodox*, two skeletal
> growths at forehead.

> > *from so simple a beginning*
> > *endless forms, most beautiful*

New bone blooded, perennially.
Our racks sized to the harvest.

> I get hungry staring at the
> hospital lawn, rife with
> testosterone; they ask what
> I've been taking.

> > *from famine and death,*
> > *the production of higher animals*

What use is a fell antler? No
longer reaching, god-struck.

> No kind of steroid, nothing
> injected. I was hiking alone
> when the pain struck—blacked
> out in the island's damp wood.

>> *grain in the balance will*
>> *determine which individual lives*

Set on your mantle, dumb
as a trophy.

> They try to make me
> comfortable. Drugged as the
> first tip breaks skin, forehead
> bloody in the morning.

>> *one law: multiply, vary, let*
>> *the strongest live*

How does your mate know
your chances of survival?

> I antler, the way a cutting
> grows new stem. Cover myself
> and leave before they claim
> what is left of my human.

>> *it inevitably follows,*
>> *as new species are formed,*

Brood Awakening

The cloud of cells awakens, intensified, swarms.
(Robert Bly)

Our bodies sexed to the land,
proliferate.

> Walk where I match the land,
> branched and lonely. The forest
> carries on past night, shelters
> what is left of me in the world.

> > *others will become rarer,*
> > *finally extinct."*

The rifle only culls
our herd.

GIRLHOOD

I was a girl starting fires with a magnifying glass,
I knew the names of things.
Then my body began towering itself toward god,

I became an archway, a hinge, public institution.
There was no language in the architecture,
only the swinging of the door and my mother's warning,

rocks thrown into a deep river. I built myself a silence,
a raft. Cowered and ran, played dead
in the water where my mother's stones rested.

What I had was a name, given to me
by an aunt whose kidneys were failing.
With this I fashioned a deed to the house of my body.

All the windows were open, the doors unlocked.
In the living room, a girl with cut glass in her mouth.
In the bedroom, something I couldn't unsee.

So I took scarves from the mirrors until the walls
flooded with light. Wrote my name in ash,
through water, until it drew clean. Bees swarmed

from the mouth of creation, the jaw of my dress.
Around us, demolition: thin light through a circle,
and the blue smoke of grass.

SAD GIRL MEETS HORNED GOD

Soft woman by the ocean
eating narcissus root. Yellow flower

in her ancient crown, the hell-bent rain.
Pissing in the field, no one

here, how lonely. Near shore,
thin silver fish. In the rain, how

lovely. Lemon and wild oat grass.
Hoofprints. A many-named god

on a black horse. Daughter, one
eyebrow crooked. Laughter. May I

offer you passage? His mare, opening
stone. Persephone's crown

on the quiet shore wilting.

NO COMMENT

We've heard there's a room hooded women enter
to write dates on the wall with torn edges of fingers.
We've heard one can cipher these numbers to bodies,
to the graceless edges of some men's beds.
Is this what you call justice? If so, why not pull back
the hood. They say this room locks from the outside.
Just wondering how you got out? If you could show us,
on your body. For example, one man we publicly
shamed. He's tied up in court, if you're looking for press
credentials. How many women stand in this room?
Where do they piss and how often? Could you comment
on the man suing your spokeswoman for slander?
How close was your body to his mouth? Was his name
chosen by lottery or straws? How will you answer
if you're sued for this poem?

IN HIS DEFENCE

her body pushed itself against everything, beige
drugstore bras and fried-egg counters, and sure

we held hands, Nabokov in our backpacks,
danced in the crotch of a karaoke bar, fake nails

and big sisters' IDs, grinding, took cabs home
for free, it wasn't the worst we'd seen, our history

teacher escorting the boys to Supersexe, third day
of the class trip, we'd seen the blue vein of that boy

pop open at the rave, carried an ounce of meth
back from Niagara in our bras, we'd tumbled out

of a cab when the driver's hands turned to us,
coaxed that same teacher into extensions, all thigh

and gloss, we knew the gamble, dealing poker
for nickel candies at lunch, and late that night,

when the teacher stumbled back, it wasn't our room
he meant to enter, swearing when I peered down

from the bunk, her snore a quiet engine below,
sorry, he said then, *sorry, I just took a wrong turn.*

INFINITY

In this poem, the man is a sequence.
His body is many bodies. He has a shitty
father, and an inclination for 80 proof.
He is a cabinetmaker, a tree removal service.
The speaker in this poem could be Elm
or Dutch Elm Disease. Except, metaphors
are finite. The speaker in this poem has
a body; many bodies. These bodies go on,
through quantum systems. Violence,
triangulation. The square of a bruise $=$
$(A^2 + B^2)$. What squares this subject, (A)?
CSI Miami, Dad walking out. Boredom.
And speaker, (B)? The windshield inside
her is hit by a deer. By deer I mean (A).
The sum, according to Pythagoras,
is always the same. Infinite triangulations.
Mostly, on a couch. In some cases, futon.
A poem can be looked away from, unlike
infinity. Here, speed $\neq$ (*distance* $\times$ *time*).
Grief is a nautilus: the logarithm turns
from itself. She returns to the couch,
to silence. He is a cabinetmaker.
His body many, every, some.

NORTHEAST BLACKOUT 2003

The summer the garbage men went on strike,
the summer the pope stood on the dais

of the Canadian National Exhibition flocked
by six thousand teenagers, all the city

went dark. We found a pool with a fence
you could climb in heels. Took off skirts, let men

hold us to the blue bottom until sirens
shone, and tickets. It was the same at the train track:

glass bottles and green dusk, trying to date
each other. One D&C that summer, a circling of rapes,

boys who still showed up with 40s and changed
the music, small guys with names we carried

in our teeth. Waiting rooms at Planned Parenthood,
our notches notched: *I was here*

2003. Every pamphlet had a Kate like us.
The game at the rich friend's cottage

to hold yourself under the lake until
the green bottle passed back. Close to a drowning,

the game at home how often
we were sent away. Every Heather on every couch

as the moms tried to forgive
themselves, and the blackouts quickened.

None of us are mothers now.
All that time swimming, so many gays,

and how deftly we knelt with a razor blade
and a mirror, kissing our own bright skin,

that night the city went dark,
and every popsicle melted, while downtown

the World Youth began singing,
wishing there were a river nearby.

WHO CAN LOOK AT THE LIGHT
WHEN IT'S SO UNFLINCHING

I called him *thirsty*, first. Drinking all the light he could find in bottles, anything anyone would buy him and mine, too. Gathering us to his hem and shouting into the night like he knew its name. *Hunter*, I called him when I woke later, tangled in light, a strange flicker of myself, with hands on my neck, gently. I liked being there, or I would have different roads walked. There was a cat named Dog, near-blind, and we loved it plainly, unlike each other. A porch where we rolled and smoked tobacco, yellowed and drank under thunder. There I called him *maker* for the way my body grew. While they muttered *drunk* in the changing light, *deadbeat* once he left. I always knew who he was. The kind of man who pushes himself beneath water. Back then, I walked into bad weather. It was the best way I knew to be alone.

RITE OF HOUSING

We stood under the moon in thrift slips, hair down
and frost early, plums turned to ice on the trees.
There I was, with a doll made of corn husks, chewing
on rosemary and asking the unseen for an apartment,
a cabin, an RV. Rachel poured salt in a circle around us,
still bleeding from her miscarriage. Like she painted dusk
for our gathering, its colour a smear on a woman's thigh.
I knew her breath and Sara's, felt it on my neck as we
leaned together and chanted. Whose daughters were we,
almost kissing as we called in land. A van where Rachel
could sleep till spring, and a husky for Sara. One blue eye,
like our friend in that half-light. You don't need a witness,
but it is good to call together. Hair of our arms rising
under the whistle of cold. We gave up begging, together.
It was enough to stand in those woods and speak.

REVIVAL

The preacher's son, behind the cabin pissing on raspberries.
Who fell off the chin of a mountain, whose spine broke like
a tooth. The preacher's son who runs the road to the ocean,
swims in shark water. Who lifts me like a cup, his mouth cold
as river, body a mountain to fall from. His body, illuminated
on the church steps as the crowd blushes. His father pointing
to the vertebrae. His father pointing to the red-lipped scar.
Faith changes the body. By the cabin, the miracle in him lifts.
He stands, drinks in the gathered light. Sees the fruit redden,
warm with ammonia. Watches my mouth when I ask him how.

HOMESTEAD

We borrowed a farmhouse and grew a glory of armpit hair.
Yard-high with yarrow, thigh-high with silk, uninvited
to the wedding down the road. What they'd call peculiar,
at the punch bowl, gas station. Queer as unbelonging.
Queer as the oak leans and moss invites itself in. We left
the city without a driver's licence. The roof full of crows.
A hive, a coop, a barrel of rain. Slow-dancing between
appetizers with my hand on your silk. They ask us politely
to leave. Queer as in trespass. As in *all of god's creatures*.
Outside, you can hear a goat opening a universe.
My sister's hands on Pluto, turning. There is a black hole
humming in a high school, in a drugstore nearby.
Nobody gets out of themselves alive. We look to Venus,
count names we can touch. Poplar, bulrush, homestead.
Crescent, willow, dyke. You don't get to take it with you,
the sign reads: you might as well dance now.

LIMIT INVOLVING INFINITY

I kissed a solider five years AWOL, white owl overhead.
They water-boarded him in training, still
he carried me into the sea.

Some men are so gentle, in the pine forest. In the shower
in Rio de Janeiro, MOM tattooed on bicep.

I have been floated to dolphins, miles from shore.
Wept and risen. Peter's spine that is no longer cracked.
Michael with conch, singing up dawn.

Michael who did not make it.

The day he drowned, I lay in the pine forest. Busted tail light,
broken car. I could not hold it all.

The soldier took me swimming, grey hawks overhead.

Some men, in the garden. In the Mexican rehab, drinking ibogaine,
FOREVER tattooed on bicep.

James sleeps with his hands in my hair, plans to foster children.

I believe there is a way to be found.
Down by the water, twins crowning.

Their sober father, the baffling sea.

SAD GIRL RETURNS TO THE LIVING

Soft woman by the bank
of the Styx. Naked in the slow

dark water to bathe. An antler crown,
a good full belly. No one here,

how lovely. A many-named god
has loved her, she's had no joy

to face. Persephone, the onrushing
river. How lonely here,

how sweet.

LETTER TO SELF AT 16

Our body has always wanted a place at the table.

*

Grace is the shattered light.

A clipboard tells us to go on—the other side; we've seen
sand become glass, in Emergency. As children, we were surrounded

by proclivity, winged ideation, a beer-canned yard. As children,
the hospital runneths

to the sea. Stitches in the face, a towel red of us
in the playground. It stays there, like a car in the amygdala

even as spring fades. *How often?* Grace—*Perceptual Dysregulation.*
Despite the kind mother,

us ghost of a girl.

*

Those before us did not have homes,
they had apothecaries.

Not one believed in the light.

& they burned them for it.

Our lungs will forgive the tinfoil.

*

In the fable, we are the axe.

There is a photograph of us titled   *field at night.*

Thinness could break us, our wings make us
mythic, I mean thighs, I mean starving.

We wear lipstick, a fake fur coat. Twelve in the woods
where is that back house

on chicken legs that wanders,

dancing hut—*Yaga's, Ingti's.* Here is our   rite of passage.

*

     O sister   *down in the river*

        —Maria.
        —In denim, water to your knees.
         Our hospital runneths
              to the sea.

*

Grief suspends time in our body.

In the fable, we split the wolf.

The first rule of girlhood is cigarettes.
We are the wood chip. BB gun, all thigh.

Vasilisa faces an impossible task.
She has to carry fire back in a dead squirrel's skull.

The second rule of girlhood is rapture.
In the fable, each of us survives.

There is a photograph titled   *field at dawn*.
We are the pile of corn husks, the sorting.

Have you heard this one? Baba Yaga can detach
her hands from her body.

Vasilisa is not a metaphor.
Vasilisa goes free.

*

O sister   down in the river   down in the river to pray

    —Maria.
    —How often? In denim. We must go on, your clipboard

       sits in the river. There is no other side.
       The joke wants to know if we can

       walk back to the bus. Our quarters winging,
       blue-cut morning   *go on,*

       You'd have been the loved field at dawn.

We find a way to go on—estuary, brackish.

*

Apothecaries, sanctums.

Those before us did not have jobs,
they had initiations

& still do.

*

Us, we were how they read the future   a cloak of bees
no singularity—
high on mellifica,
the Greeks
shattered   O sister   called us Graces.

Wax: light hardened, light made soft again.
Ancient geometry: the hexagon opens, epigenetically.

In our mouth   go on   life reforms again.

Autogenesis

There is one masterpiece, the hexagonal cell
(Maurice Maeterlinck)

*

The bathtub in the garden is filled with bees / clinging to rose honey
spun by their mouths and stolen / I call them here / as instrument /
and lay the man / into the barbed ceramic tub / humming /
I am trying to forgive you / I shout though drones lick his ears /
and when he rises / blessed by ten thousand stings
I offer barrels of water caught under winter / wash yourself /
I order though / he does not know I'm here
stands under taps and rinses / as if alone / alone / this morning
it helps / to study pain inside the other / and know
he forced me / thrumming / to where he already stood.

—overture

In the garden, a queen breaks hexagon to flower, to find the mites
abound. The singular

erases itself, not into marriage
but the natural law of slut: contagion,

creation.

             —nothing exists for itself alone (Darwin)

The Graces drank *kykion*, spiked honey—held drones
to each other's brows. A mad girl's blessing,

to channel at the comb: oracular, their joy unknown
to the living. At night, no woman claimed them,

they let the unchained in.

Our family tells the story of a pancreas
in Northern Ontario. It expands, contracts

with prayer. Great-Aunt Rebecca lives
by the grace of the word

and that word lives in the good pine room
downtown. You can smell Lake Timiskaming

through the window.

Your arms always filled with gifts (Hail Mary)

Our grandmother's sister was a nun named Mary. Once, she saw
my sister dance barefoot in High Park. *Contemporary performance,*

my sister lifted her hands to the cherry blossoms
as if sinning. I have found myself

that blooded. It began at thirteen and went on,
lifting my hands in the blue night.

Full of grace; grace spilling (Hail Mary)

Rebecca's daughters are truck drivers who never
married. I look like the eldest, except

for my mouth. I believe in a cellular god, the glass slide
under a blinking microscope. I believe

in a belief in the light, and also that women
are quietly loving women in passenger seats

at truck stops. Illumination can be
blinding. That day on the mountain, Mary; my hands

in the grass of a good woman's hair.

Alive with Holy beauty (Hail Mary)

Water and lace   pockets of salt
rosemary   in dry fields at dark
walk the circle   heat rising from hands
what you might call steam a reddening light
rose scarves   a dozen wings lifting

the bower bright   & beckoning

Deeply I breathe your roses (Hail Mary)

My friends wash each other's feet on camera,

listen bedside, survive in sex. To own a name
is to own a wig, anyway. What I know of Magdalene

I know of love. Bright morning in the diner, hot fries
the colour of dawn, we touch

each other's brows with water.

Sweet advocate of sinners (Hail Magdalene)

In hospital, my friend Mary is raised in bed like a prayer,
and her father is knitting

a narrow scarf. Liver in sepsis, red as a plastic cup
when I picture it, under my arbutus,

in silence.

My cat seeks out the same black snake
every morning. It bends into a perfect circle

and she takes it in her mouth. Then?

Then it goes free.

Unity in Trinity, World without End (Hail Magdalene)

In *Droughtland, Oregon*, ninety witches pray
at the trunk of a oak tree. Crones

in nuclear grief: *forgive us our plutonium, DDT.*

Elders who handcuffed themselves to fences,
weeping tear gas, as power plants rose

in the Bay. They slept it off in jail, set their sigils
by wire light. The right hand casts,

left binds quietly: *may none lay claim to hydrogen.*

Chanting as a woman's eyes rapture, roll back sober,
and that night, midnight—it finally rains.

Who before darkness wast restored (Hail Magdalene)

By that same oak, a near-mother kneeling.
Seven months pregnant as tumours are found in her lungs—

forgive us our Lanthium, DDT.

What is remembered lives   in us as in soil.

May prayers be made

     in the name of Mary
     in the name of Mary   *hear us*
                               pray for us

& her child lives.

Now and at the hour of our death (Hail Magdalene)

Watch, now: a girl weeps into water, as if kissing the stream.
And the stream runs down the mountain.

In silence, lightning hits the ocean
and becomes phosphorescence.

I'm lying, the way good women lie—(Liturgy);
sand becomes glass this way.

There are food stamps in America,
hysterectomies, class action law suits—(Litany);

people find a way.

A white owl perches in our driveway
in a dumb shaft of sunlight.

I believe you, you said.

My lungs like a broken violin
in the tire fire of downtown.

I did not know what pain was,
and then I did.

The legislature tells us to have faith.
Oxycodone, Pain Industrial Complex—(Eulogy);

there is power in prayer. A parking lot
presses its palms together and sings.

Retrogenesis, regenesis:
some lizards self-actualize their young.

In the realm of bacteria, all law is gone.

In the morning, a yellow flower
blossoms from your ear.

Pulses, unfolds as I watch it.
You sleep deeply, curled on your side,

lips parted as if to speak.
The smell of pollen so rich, I expect

bees to surround the cabin.
Both of us naked, I think maybe

they'll swarm or walk across our skin
like a living blanket. And you will lie

still as honey until one slips onto
your tongue, only wake as you swallow

its sweet-blooded sting. I watch for
an hour, tempted to break the stem,

place it in a jar on my nightstand
like a sugar trap. Instead, fall back

to sleep, hands light on your lips,
trying to keep out the bees.

It started when you were a kid. Left ear infected
twice a season, nothing could drain it

properly, and who can afford all the doctors?
The eardrum ruptured like a storm at dawn.

Like your mother shattering a window.
Deafness was the first room no one could break into.

You spat yellow medicine into the sink;
prayed the silence would grow.

It started when I was a kid. Three weeks of macaroni
salad, antipsychotics, cold recycled air.

A blond girl clutched her cross, still shaking from ECT.
Beside me: endless dawn, her wiped amygdala.

She prayed from the vinyl couch like a Mary,
and I lied my way free, even as I witnessed

a yellow flower rise from the prescription
on my new doctor's desk.

At dusk, a hawk drops
a squirrel's rib cage at our feet,

picked so clean the bones are yellow.
I wrap it in silk, light a candle

in the cabin where I am unmaking my life.

This is the gift of a half-broken body:
you relearn everything.

At world's end, we hold a willow branch.
In cold green water, wading toward Graces.

Oracles in denim, oracles stripped down.

It is time for two-hand magic,
the circle cast both ways.

Our mouth, a yellow flower.
Our mouth, our mind, our kin.

Infinity is not a noun.
The speed of light is the same as the speed of gravity.

At the base of an oak tree, acorns.
A white squirrel digs his implausible home.

I forgive you, I tell my hands.

I forgive you, future—(Benediction);
Together, the joke goes, we have made God laugh.

In the garden, a maiden queen arises to finds her drones
abound. After the death

of monocrop in the valley; no more sweet glyphosate breeze,
her sex begets an ecosystem. Contagion,

creation, *trophic cascade.*

> O see thy colonies lifting, queen.
> O find thy way back home.

I will arise and go now, and go to Innisfree,
And a small cabin build there, of clay and wattles made:
Nine bean-rows will I have there, a hive for the honey-bee;
And live alone in the bee-loud glade.

(William Butler Yeats)

*

Up on the hill, mist. Two vultures circle,
looking for snakes in damp grass.

A girl in red contemplates the snakes.
Her story moves slowly, the way love ends.

In summer, the bluffs will dry yellow
and tinder, in summer when she is alone.

At school they cut dandelions, and bees
stumbled too drunk to bite. Back then,

the city didn't understand its cycles.
The girl is a woman who splits hives slowly,

to protect the eggs at the centre. In summer,
she'll leave the honey, heavy on the comb.

In her red dress, that girl is humming.
The way stories end, on a hilltop, slowly.

Black snake in the mouth of the celebrant bird.

Acknowledgements

These poems were created while living throughout the unceded, ancestral, occupied lands of the Coast Salish peoples, including the lands of the of the Musqueam, Tsleil-Waututh, Skwxwú7mesh, Cowichan, Chemainus, and WSANEC (Tsawout, Tsartlip, Pauquachin, Tseycum) First Nations, as a visitor to Treaty 7 Territory, and the islands of the Hawaiian people. I will continue to strive for my work to be in service to the past, present, and future of these living lands and their ecosystems, as a settler and uninvited visitor to these territories.

Profound gratitude goes to Karen Solie, the editor of this collection, who has been with these poems from the beginning. This collection discovered its possibilities under her keen and caring eye. Gratitude also goes to Ocean Vuong, the first reader of *Postcards for my Sister,* Colette Bryce, Ken Babstock, and Kyo Maclear for mentorship, inspiration, and editorial advice during the development of this book, as well as to my long-standing first readers, Esther McPhee and Ellie Sawatzky. A heartfelt thanks to Book*hug for believing in my vision, and trusting the journey of this book.

This book was made possible through the support of the Canada Council for the Arts, the BC Arts Council, the Banff Centre, the Writers' Trust of Canada, and CBC Books. Poems from this collection first appeared in *enRoute Magazine*, *Room Magazine*, *Arc Poetry Magazine*, *CV2*, and *Poetry Is Dead.* I am grateful to the editors, jurors, and literary organizations that saw a place for these poems. Thank you for your support, and for the support you give to poetry in Canada. A special thank-you to CBC Books, Stephanie Sinclair, the Canadian spoken word community, my teachers and workshop circles, the Writers' Trust and Carolyn Smart, founder of the RBC Bronwen Wallace Award. In Bronwen Wallace's words: *you move in your own seasons, through the seasons of others.* It is an honour to be part of the ongoing legacy of Bronwen Wallace's work in the world.

A note on process: *Creationisms* uses a combination of direct quotations and adapted source material collected from *On the Origin of Species* by Charles Darwin, *Exodus 10* from the New King James translation of the Bible, and statements published on Monsanto's website, including their official statement: *Glyphosate Does Not Cause Cancer.* Additionally, "It's About Survival" is composed of adapted quotations from an interview I conducted with beekeeper Ian Smyth of *Hives for Humanity*, for an article entitled "Rare Honey" (*Briarpatch Magazine*, Spring 2014). "Deforestation" quotes ecologist Mark E. McConnaughay, and uses colonial place names to depict specific historical events related to Lyme disease. Throughout these poems, lines in italics have been reordered and spliced for recontextualization. The original quotations are readily available, and interpretation is intended to be the reader's own.

Finally, *grazie infinite* to James McCarthy, for living these poems with me; to my mother, Christine Jackson, for sending me on this path; and Elysia Glover, for acting as midwife to this book. Thank you to my sisters, Teoma and Gabrielle; to my aunts, ancestors, and incredible mentors—Sheri-D Wilson, Seraphina Capranos, and Robert Birch. To my coven and chosen family, dear friends, and co-creators—Jen, Jack, Aaron, Tanya, Barbara, Alyssa, Elyse, Paula, Savannah, Fennec, Aly, Saera, Tamara, Ananda, Marla, Charlie, Jillian, Chandra, Moe, Esther and Ellie, and all those I've dreamed beside: I believe in the future we are practicing. And last but not least, *grazie mille* to the keystone of this book, *apis millefera,* the western honeybee.

JACKLYN ATLAS

Alessandra Naccarato is the recipient of the 2015 RBC Bronwen Wallace Award for Emerging Writers and the winner of the 2017 CBC Poetry Prize. A two-time finalist for *Arc Magazine*'s Poem of Year and the Edna Steabler Personal Essay Prize, she holds an MFA in Creative Writing from the University of British Columbia, and has toured nationally and internationally as a spoken word artist. She is based between Toronto, Ontario and Salt Spring Island, British Columbia. *Re-Origin of Species* is her debut poetry collection.

Colophon

Manufactured as the first edition of
Re-Origin of Species
in the fall of 2019 by Book*hug Press

Edited for the press by Karen Solie
Copy edited by Stuart Ross
Design and typography Gareth Lind / Lind Design
Cover photo: iStock.com/Pattadis Walarput
Typeset in Filosofia, designed by Zuzana Licko, 1996

bookhugpress.ca